ٱللَّهُ عَلَيْهِ وَسَلَّمَ

وَبَيانُ مَعْناها وَكَيْفِيّتِها وَشَيْءٍ مِمّا أُلِّفَ فِيها

The Virtue of Sending Ṣalāt Upon the Prophet ﷺ

Along with clarification of its meaning, its manner, and a glimpse at what has been authored surrounding it

By Shaykh al-ʿAllāmah

ʿAbd al-Muḥsin ibn Ḥamad al-ʿAbbād al-Badr

حفظه الله

First Edition: Dhū al-Qa'dah 1444H/ June 2023CE

ISBN: 979-8-218-16406-5

Translation: Abū Suhayl Anwar Wright

Reviewed by:

Z. bint Ahmed

Abū Sa'eed Mohamed

Mohamed Elamin Kouar

Contact:

Twitter: @anwarphilly

عَزَّوَجَلَّ	The Mighty and Majestic.
سُبْحَانَهُۥوَتَعَالَىٰ	The Sublime and Exalted.
صَلَّىٰٱللَّهُعَلَيْهِوَسَلَّمَ	May Allāh make good mention of His Prophet in the highest company and grant him safety in this life and the next.
رَضِيَٱللَّهُعَنْهُ	May Allāh be pleased with him.
رَحِمَهُٱللَّهُ	May Allāh show mercy to him.
عَلَيْهِٱلسَّلَامُ	Peace be upon him.

Table of Contents

Introduction 1

When is Worship Accepted? 6

The Meaning of Ṣalāt Upon the Prophet (صَلَّى ٱللَّهُ عَلَيْهِ وَسَلَّمَ) 10

The Meaning of Taslīm Upon the Prophet (صَلَّى ٱللَّهُ عَلَيْهِ وَسَلَّمَ) 13

The Manner of Sending Ṣalāt Upon the Prophet (صَلَّى ٱللَّهُ عَلَيْهِ وَسَلَّمَ) 14

The Best and Most Complete Manner of Sending Ṣalāt Upon the Prophet (صَلَّى ٱللَّهُ عَلَيْهِ وَسَلَّمَ) 19

Two Abridged Versions of Sending Ṣalāt and Salām Upon Him (صَلَّى ٱللَّهُ عَلَيْهِ وَسَلَّمَ) 21

The Virtue of Sending Ṣalāt Upon the Prophet (صَلَّى ٱللَّهُ عَلَيْهِ وَسَلَّمَ) 24

A Glimpse at Some Treatises Authored Surrounding Ṣalāt Upon the Prophet (صَلَّى ٱللَّهُ عَلَيْهِ وَسَلَّمَ) 30

Innovated Manners of Supplication Found in the Book *Dalā'il al-Khayrāt* 35

Some Examples of Fabricated Aḥādīth in the Book *Dalā'il al-Khayrāt* 39

The Great Status of the Sunnah Among the Salaf and a Clarification of Why They Were Victorious Over Their Enemies, Contrary to the Condition of the Muslims Today 42

بِسْمِ ٱللَّهِ ٱلرَّحْمَٰنِ ٱلرَّحِيمِ

Introduction

All praise is due to Allāh, Lord of all creation. The Most Merciful, the Bestower of mercy and the Owner of the Day of Judgment. O Allāh, raise the mention of Muḥammad and the family of Muḥammad, just as You raised the mention of Ibrāhīm and the family of Ibrāhīm; You are the One full of praise, full of glory. O Allāh, bestow blessings upon Muḥammad and upon the family of Muḥammad, just as You bestowed blessings upon Ibrāhīm and upon the family of Ibrāhīm; You are the One full of praise, full of glory. O Allāh, be pleased with the noble Companions and those who follow them in goodness.

Indeed, the blessings of Allāh, the Most High, upon His servants are many and innumerable. The greatest blessing which Allāh has bestowed upon the jinn and mankind is that He sent to them His servant, Messenger, and intimate friend; His beloved, and the elect from His creation, Muḥammad (صَلَّىٰ ٱللَّهُ عَلَيْهِ وَسَلَّمَ). This was so that He —by [sending] him— could deliver them from the depths of darkness to light, and remove them from the humiliation of worshiping the creation, to the honor of worshipping the Creator (سُبْحَانَهُ وَتَعَالَىٰ). Also, that he may direct them to the path of salvation and happiness and warn them from the paths of destruction and wretchedness.

Surely, Allāh lauded this tremendous and immense blessing in His Mighty Book. He said:

﴿لَقَدْ مَنَّ ٱللَّهُ عَلَى ٱلْمُؤْمِنِينَ إِذْ بَعَثَ فِيهِمْ رَسُولًا مِّنْ أَنفُسِهِمْ يَتْلُوا۟ عَلَيْهِمْ ءَايَـٰتِهِۦ وَيُزَكِّيهِمْ وَيُعَلِّمُهُمُ ٱلْكِتَـٰبَ وَٱلْحِكْمَةَ وَإِن كَانُوا۟ مِن قَبْلُ لَفِى ضَلَـٰلٍ مُّبِينٍ ﴿١٦٤﴾﴾

"Indeed Allāh conferred a great favor on the believers when He sent among them a Messenger (Muḥammad) from among themselves, reciting unto them His Verses (the Qur'ān), and purifying them (from sins by their following him), and instructing them (in) the Book (the Qur'ān) and Al-Ḥikmah [the wisdom and the Sunnah of the Prophet (i.e. his legal ways, statements, acts of worship, etc.)], while before that they had been in manifest error."
Āl-'Imrān 3:164

And He (سُبْحَانَهُ وَتَعَالَىٰ) said:

﴿هُوَ ٱلَّذِىٓ أَرْسَلَ رَسُولَهُۥ بِٱلْهُدَىٰ وَدِينِ ٱلْحَقِّ لِيُظْهِرَهُۥ عَلَى ٱلدِّينِ كُلِّهِۦ ۚ وَكَفَىٰ بِٱللَّهِ شَهِيدًا ﴿٢٨﴾﴾

"He it is Who has sent His Messenger (Muḥammad) with guidance and the religion of truth (Islām), that He may make it (Islām) superior over all religions. And All-Sufficient is Allāh as a Witness." Al-Fatḥ 48:28

Indeed, he (عليه أفضل الصلاة والسلام) conveyed the Message, fulfilled the trust [given to him by Allāh], and gave sincere advice to the

Ummah in the most perfect and complete manner. He gave glad tidings and warnings, directed to all good and warned from all evil.

Allāh the Most High revealed to him while he was standing on 'Arafah —not long before he died (صَلَّى ٱللَّهُ عَلَيْهِ وَسَلَّمَ)— His saying, the Most High:

﴿ٱلْيَوْمَ أَكْمَلْتُ لَكُمْ دِينَكُمْ وَأَتْمَمْتُ عَلَيْكُمْ نِعْمَتِى وَرَضِيتُ لَكُمُ ٱلْإِسْلَٰمَ دِينًا ۚ ٣﴾

"This day, I have perfected your religion for you, completed My Favor upon you, and have chosen for you Islām as your religion." Al-Māidah 5:3

Furthermore, he (صَلَّى ٱللَّهُ عَلَيْهِ وَسَلَّمَ) was extremely eager for the Ummah's happiness, just as Allāh the Most High said, praising those virtuous qualities that He favored him with:

﴿لَقَدْ جَآءَكُمْ رَسُولٌ مِّنْ أَنفُسِكُمْ عَزِيزٌ عَلَيْهِ مَا عَنِتُّمْ حَرِيصٌ
عَلَيْكُم بِٱلْمُؤْمِنِينَ رَءُوفٌ رَّحِيمٌ ١٢٨﴾

"Verily, there has come unto you a Messenger (Muḥammad) from amongst yourselves (i.e. whom you know well). It grieves him that you should receive any injury or difficulty. He (Muḥammad) is anxious over you (to be rightly guided, to repent to Allāh, and beg Him to pardon and forgive your sins, in order that you may enter Paradise and be saved from the punishment of the Hell-fire), for the believers (he is) full of pity, kind, and merciful." Al-Taubah 9:128

And these tasks that he undertook (صَلَّى ٱللَّهُ عَلَيْهِ وَسَلَّمَ): conveying the Message, fulfilling the trust [given to him by Allāh], and giving sincere advice to the Ummah; this is the Ummah's right upon him, as Allāh (سُبْحَانَهُۥ وَتَعَالَىٰ) said:

﴿ وَمَا عَلَى ٱلرَّسُولِ إِلَّا ٱلْبَلَٰغُ ٱلْمُبِينُ ﴿٥٤﴾ ﴾

"The Messenger's duty is only to convey (the Message) in a clear way (i.e. to preach in a plain way)." Al-Nūr 24:54

And He said:

﴿ فَهَلْ عَلَى ٱلرُّسُلِ إِلَّا ٱلْبَلَٰغُ ٱلْمُبِينُ ﴿٣٥﴾ ﴾

"Then! Are the Messengers charged with anything but to clearly convey the Message?" Al-Naḥl 16:35

Also, Imām al-Bukhārī reported in his Ṣaḥīḥ on the authority of al-Zuhrī who said:

"From Allāh is the Message, upon the Messenger is to convey, and upon us is to submit."

Subsequently, a sign of a Muslim's happiness is that he yields and submits to what the Messenger of Allāh (صَلَّى ٱللَّهُ عَلَيْهِ وَسَلَّمَ) has come with, as Allāh (سُبْحَانَهُۥ وَتَعَالَىٰ) stated:

﴿ فَلَا وَرَبِّكَ لَا يُؤْمِنُونَ حَتَّىٰ يُحَكِّمُوكَ فِيمَا شَجَرَ بَيْنَهُمْ ثُمَّ لَا يَجِدُوا۟ فِىٓ
أَنفُسِهِمْ حَرَجًا مِّمَّا قَضَيْتَ وَيُسَلِّمُوا۟ تَسْلِيمًا ﴿٦٥﴾ ﴾

"But no, by your Lord, they can have no Faith, until they make you (O Muḥammad) judge in all disputes between them, and find in themselves no resistance against your decisions, and accept (them) with full submission." Al-Nisā' 4:65

And He, the Most High, stated:

﴿وَمَا كَانَ لِمُؤْمِنٍ وَلَا مُؤْمِنَةٍ إِذَا قَضَى ٱللَّهُ وَرَسُولُهُۥٓ أَمْرًا أَن يَكُونَ لَهُمُ ٱلْخِيَرَةُ مِنْ أَمْرِهِمْ ۗ وَمَن يَعْصِ ٱللَّهَ وَرَسُولَهُۥ فَقَدْ ضَلَّ ضَلَٰلًا مُّبِينًا ﴿٣٦﴾﴾

"It is not for a believer, man or woman, when Allāh and His Messenger have decreed a matter that they should have any option in their decision. And whoever disobeys Allāh and His Messenger, he has indeed strayed in a plain error." Al-Aḥzāb 33:36

And He the Most High said:

﴿فَلْيَحْذَرِ ٱلَّذِينَ يُخَالِفُونَ عَنْ أَمْرِهِۦٓ أَن تُصِيبَهُمْ فِتْنَةٌ أَوْ يُصِيبَهُمْ عَذَابٌ أَلِيمٌ ﴿٦٣﴾﴾

"And let those who oppose the Messenger's (Muḥammad) commandment (i.e. his Sunnah legal ways, orders, acts of worship, statements, etc.) (among the sects) beware, lest some Fitnah (disbelief, trials, afflictions, earthquakes, killing, overpowered by a tyrant, etc.) befall them or a painful torment be inflicted on them." Al-Nūr 24:63

When is Worship Accepted?

Worship of Allāh is accepted by Him and will be of benefit before Him if it comprises of two essential matters:

First: that the worship is done solely and sincerely for Allāh, giving no share of any of it to anyone besides Him. So, just as He, the Most High, has no partner in His Dominion, He likewise has no partner in worship. He the Most High said:

﴿وَأَنَّ ٱلْمَسَٰجِدَ لِلَّهِ فَلَا تَدْعُوا۟ مَعَ ٱللَّهِ أَحَدًا ١٨﴾

"And the mosques are for Allāh (Alone), so invoke not anyone along with Allāh." Al-Jinn 72:18

And He (تَبَارَكَ وَتَعَالَىٰ) said:

﴿قُلْ إِنَّ صَلَاتِى وَنُسُكِى وَمَحْيَاىَ وَمَمَاتِى لِلَّهِ رَبِّ ٱلْعَٰلَمِينَ ١٦٢ لَا شَرِيكَ لَهُۥ ۖ وَبِذَٰلِكَ أُمِرْتُ وَأَنَا۠ أَوَّلُ ٱلْمُسْلِمِينَ ١٦٣﴾

"Say (O Muḥammad): 'Verily, my *Ṣalāt* (prayer), my sacrifice, my living, and my dying are for Allāh, the Lord of the 'Alamin (mankind, jinns and all that exists). He has no partner. And of this I have been commanded, and I am the first of the Muslims.'" Al-An'ām 6:162-163

Second: that worship be done in accordance with the legislation that His Messenger Muḥammad (صَلَّى ٱللَّهُ عَلَيْهِ وَسَلَّمَ) came with, just as Allāh the Most High said:

﴿وَمَآ ءَاتَىٰكُمُ ٱلرَّسُولُ فَخُذُوهُ وَمَا نَهَىٰكُمۡ عَنۡهُ فَٱنتَهُواْۚ وَٱتَّقُواْ ٱللَّهَۖ إِنَّ ٱللَّهَ شَدِيدُ ٱلۡعِقَابِ ٧﴾

"And whatsoever the Messenger (Muḥammad) gives you, take it, and whatsoever he forbids you, abstain (from it) , and fear Allāh. Verily, Allāh is Severe in punishment." Al-Ḥashr 59:7

And He, the Most High, said:

﴿قُلۡ إِن كُنتُمۡ تُحِبُّونَ ٱللَّهَ فَٱتَّبِعُونِي يُحۡبِبۡكُمُ ٱللَّهُ وَيَغۡفِرۡ لَكُمۡ ذُنُوبَكُمۡۚ وَٱللَّهُ غَفُورٞ رَّحِيمٞ ٣١﴾

"Say (O Muḥammad to mankind): "If you (really) love Allāh then follow me (i.e. accept Islāmic Monotheism, follow the Qur'ān and the Sunnah), Allāh will love you and forgive you of your sins. And Allāh is Oft-Forgiving, Most Merciful." Āl-'Imrān 3:31

Also, he (صَلَّى ٱللَّهُ عَلَيْهِ وَسَلَّمَ) stated in the ḥadīth reported by al-Bukhārī and Muslim on the authority of 'Āishah (رَضِيَ ٱللَّهُ عَنْهَا):

من أحدث في أمرنا هذا ما ليس منه فهو ردٌّ

"Whoever introduces into this affair of ours (i.e. Islam) that which is not from it, it is rejected."

Also, in a narration [collected by] Muslim:

من عمل عملاً ليس عليه أمرنا فهو ردٌّ

"Whoever does an action not in accordance with our affair, it is rejected."

He (صَلَّى ٱللَّهُ عَلَيْهِ وَسَلَّمَ) also said:

عليكم بسنتي وسنّة الخلفاء الراشدين المهديين من بعدي عضُّوا عليها بالنواجذ وإياكم ومحدثات الأمور فإن كل محدثة بدعة وكل بدعة ضلالة

"Upon you is [to cling to] my Sunnah, and the Sunnah of the rightly guided Caliphs after me. Bite down upon [them both] with your molar teeth. And beware of newly invented matters, for every newly invented matter is an innovation, and every innovation is misguidance."

Therefore, since the favor of Allāh (سُبْحَانَهُ وَتَعَالَىٰ) upon the believers in sending His Messenger is so great, Allāh (سُبْحَانَهُ وَتَعَالَىٰ) commanded them in His Mighty Book to send Ṣalāt and Salām upon him. This is after He informed them that both He and His angels send Ṣalāt upon him.

He, (سُبْحَانَهُ وَتَعَالَىٰ) said:

﴿ إِنَّ ٱللَّهَ وَمَلَٰٓئِكَتَهُۥ يُصَلُّونَ عَلَى ٱلنَّبِيِّ ۚ يَٰٓأَيُّهَا ٱلَّذِينَ ءَامَنُوا۟ صَلُّوا۟ عَلَيْهِ وَسَلِّمُوا۟ تَسْلِيمًا ﴿٥٦﴾ ﴾

"Allāh sends His Ṣalāt (Graces, Honors, Blessings, Mercy, etc.) on the Prophet (Muḥammad) and also His angels too (ask Allāh to bless him). O you who believe! Send your Ṣalāt on him (Muḥammad), and (you should) greet (salute) him

with the Islāmic way of greeting (salutation i.e. Al-Salamu 'Alaikum)." Al-Aḥzāb 33:56

Also, the Prophet (صَلَّى ٱللَّٰهُ عَلَيْهِ وَسَلَّمَ) clarified in the purified Sunnah the virtue of sending Ṣalāt upon him (صَلَّى ٱللَّٰهُ عَلَيْهِ وَسَلَّمَ), its manner, and other than that from the rulings related to it.

Thus, I will speak about the meaning of sending Ṣalāt upon the Prophet (صَلَّى ٱللَّٰهُ عَلَيْهِ وَسَلَّمَ), its virtue, and clarification of its manner. Afterwards, I will give a glimpse of some of the books authored surrounding this act of worship.

I ask Allāh, the Most High, for success and correctness.

The Meaning of Ṣalāt Upon the Prophet (ﷺ)

Allāh's Ṣalāt upon His Prophet (ﷺ) has been explained as His extolling him among the angels. As for the Ṣalāt of the angels upon him, it has been explained to mean their supplication (du'ā') for him. This explanation has been reported from Abū al-'Āliyah, as al-Bukhārī relayed from him in his Ṣaḥīḥ at the beginning of the chapter:

﴿ إِنَّ ٱللَّهَ وَمَلَٰٓئِكَتَهُۥ يُصَلُّونَ عَلَى ٱلنَّبِيِّ ۚ يَٰٓأَيُّهَا ٱلَّذِينَ ءَامَنُوا۟ صَلُّوا۟ عَلَيْهِ وَسَلِّمُوا۟ تَسْلِيمًا ﴿٥٦﴾ ﴾

"Allāh sends His Ṣalāt (Graces, Honors, Blessings, Mercy, etc.) on the Prophet (Muḥammad) and also His angels too (ask Allāh to bless him). O you who believe! Send your Ṣalāt on him (Muḥammad), and (you should) greet (salute) him with the Islāmic way of greeting (salutation i.e. Al-Sālamu 'Alaikum)." Al-Aḥzāb 33:56

Also, regarding the explanation of the Ṣalāt of the angels upon him, al-Bukhārī said after mentioning the explanation of Abū al-'Āliyah: Ibn 'Abbās said: "[the meaning of] 'they send Ṣalāt' is: *Yubarrikūna*; meaning, they supplicate for blessings (al-barakah) for him."

Also, the Ṣalāt of Allāh upon him has been explained to mean forgiveness and mercy, as al-Ḥāfiẓ ibn Ḥajar conveyed in *al-Fatḥ* from a number [of scholars]. Afterwards, he critiqued that explanation and said "The foremost of those statements is what has preceded from Abū al-'Āliyah, that the meaning of Allāh's Ṣalāt upon His Prophet is His extolling him and declaring his greatness; and the Ṣalāt of the angels and others upon him is their seeking that Allāh, the Most High, does that. Meaning, they seek that [Allāh] *increases* this [for the Prophet], not that they seek the basis of [Allāh's] Ṣalāt [upon him].

Al-Ḥāfiẓ also stated: "Al-Ḥalīmī stated in *al-Shu'ab*: 'The meaning of Ṣalāt upon the Prophet (ﷺ) is glorification [of him]. Therefore, the meaning of our statement 'O Allāh, send Ṣalat upon Muḥammad' is: glorify Muḥammad; and what is meant is that he be glorified in this world by raising his mention, making his religion apparent, and preserving his sharī'ah. As for the Hereafter [it means] magnifying his reward, allowing him to intercede for his Ummah, and displaying his excellence by way of the praiseworthy standing (i.e. al-Maqām al-Maḥmūd). Based on this, the meaning of Allāh's statement, the Most High:

﴿ صَلُّوا۟ عَلَيْهِ ﴾

'Send Ṣalāt upon him'

is invoke your Lord that He sends Ṣalāt upon him.'"

Al-'Allāmah Ibn al-Qayyim stated in his book *Jilā al-Afhām Fī al-Ṣalāt wa al-Salām 'Alā Khayr al-Anām*, regarding Allāh and His angels' Ṣalāt upon His Messenger (ﷺ), and His command to His believing slaves to send Ṣalāt upon him; following his rejection of its meaning to be "mercy" and "seeking forgiveness [for him]", he mentions: "Rather, the Ṣalāt which has been commanded with therein (i.e. meaning the verse in Sūrah al-Aḥzāb) is requesting from Allāh that which He informed us of regarding His Ṣalāt and that of His angels [upon the Prophet]; meaning, extolling him, bringing his virtue and nobility to light, and [Allāh] wanting to honor him and bring him close. Thus, in [the verse] is a statement and a request. Furthermore, He named the asking and supplication that occurs on our part "Ṣalāt", and this is for two reasons:

First: It entails praise [of the Prophet] from the one sending Ṣalāt upon him, as well as proclaiming his nobility and virtue. Also, [it entails] the fact that Allāh wants and loves that [to occur]. Therefore [the verse] implies a statement and a request.

Two: It has been named "Ṣalāt" due to our asking Allāh to send Ṣalāt upon [the Prophet]. Therefore, Allāh's Ṣalāt upon him is His extolling [him] in order to elevate his mention and bring him close. As for our Ṣalāt upon him, [then it is] our asking Allāh the Most High to fulfill and complete [those actions] regarding him."

The Meaning of Taslīm Upon the Prophet (صَلَّى ٱللَّهُ عَلَيْهِ وَسَلَّمَ)

As for the meaning of Taslīm upon the Prophet (صَلَّى ٱللَّهُ عَلَيْهِ وَسَلَّمَ), al-Majd al-Fīrūz Ābādī stated in his book *Al-Ṣilāt wa al-Bushar Fī al-Ṣalāt 'Alā Khayr al-Bashar*: "Its meaning is that al-Salām—which is one of the names of Allāh the Most High—be upon you [O Prophet]. Thus, its interpretation would be: may you never be void of goodness (khayrāt) and blessings (barakāt), and may you always be safe from harm and misfortune.

This is because the name of Allāh, the Most High, is only mentioned on matters with the hope that sentiments of goodness and blessings are gathered within them, while deficiencies and flaws are banished from them.

Furthermore, it is possible that al-Salām means al-Salāmah (i.e. well-being). Meaning, let Allāh's (سُبْحَانَهُ وَتَعَالَىٰ) decree upon you be al-Salāmah; meaning that you be free from blame and deficiencies.

Therefore, when you say:

اللَّهُمَّ سَلِّمْ عَلَى مُحَمَّدٍ

O Allāh send Salām upon Muḥammad

What you intend by that is: O Allāh, decree for Muḥammad in his call [to Islām], his Ummah, and in his mention, protection (Salāmah) from every flaw. Thus, as time passes, his call will become more prominent and widespread, his Ummah will continue to grow, and his mention will continue to elevate."

The Manner of Sending Ṣalāt Upon the Prophet (ﷺ)

As for the manner of sending Ṣalāt upon the Prophet (ﷺ), the Messenger of Allāh (ﷺ) already clarified this to his Companions when they asked him concerning that. This manner has been reported from many different routes of transmission from a number of the Companions (رَضِيَ اللَّهُ عَنْهُمْ). Here I will mention what is found in the two Ṣaḥīḥs, or just one of them:

[Imām] al-Bukhārī reported in the "Book of Prophets" within his Ṣaḥīḥ on the authority of 'Abd al-Raḥmān ibn Abī Laylā who said: "Ka'b ibn 'Ujrah met me and said: 'Shall I not gift you with a gift that I heard from the Prophet (ﷺ)?' I said: Yes, gift it to me. He said: 'I asked the Messenger of Allāh (ﷺ), saying: O Messenger of Allāh, how do we send Ṣalāt upon you and your family? Allāh has already taught us how to send Salām upon you. He said: 'Say:

اللَّهُمَّ صَلِّ عَلَى مُحَمَّدٍ وَعَلَى آلِ مُحَمَّدٍ كَمَا صَلَّيْتَ عَلَى إِبْرَاهِيمَ وَعَلَى آلِ إِبْرَاهِيمَ
إِنَّكَ حَمِيْدٌ مَجِيْدٌ اللَّهُمَّ بَارِكْ عَلَى مُحَمَّدٍ وَعَلَى آلِ مُحَمَّدٍ كَمَا بَارَكْتَ عَلَى إِبْرَاهِيمَ
وَعَلَى آلِ إِبْرَاهِيمَ إِنَّكَ حَمِيْدٌ مَجِيْدٌ

O Allāh send Ṣalāt upon Muḥammad and the family of Muḥammad, just as You sent Ṣalāt upon Ibrāhīm and the family of Ibrāhīm, You are the One full of praise, full of glory. O Allāh bestow blessings upon Muḥammad and the family of Muḥammad, just as You bestowed blessings upon Ibrāhīm and the family of Ibrāhīm, You are the One full of praise, full of glory.'"

He also collected the ḥadīth of Ka'b ibn 'Ujrah in the Chapter of Tafsīr within his Ṣaḥīḥ under the Tafsīr of Sūrah al-Aḥzāb. Its wording is:

"It was said, O Messenger of Allāh, we already know how to send Salām upon you, so how do we send Ṣalāt upon you?" He said: 'Say:

اللَّهُمَّ صَلِّ عَلَى مُحَمَّدٍ وَعَلَى آلِ مُحَمَّدٍ كَمَا صَلَّيْتَ عَلَى آلِ إِبْرَاهِيمَ إِنَّكَ حَمِيْدٌ مَجِيْدٌ

اللَّهُمَّ بَارِكْ على مُحَمَّدٍ وَعَلَى آلِ مُحَمَّدٍ كَمَا بَارَكْتَ على آلِ إِبْرَاهِيمَ إِنَّكَ حَمِيْدٌ مَجِيْدٌ

O Allāh send Ṣalāt upon Muḥammad and the family of Muḥammad, just as You sent Ṣalāt upon the family of Ibrāhīm, You are the One full of praise, full of glory. O Allāh bestow blessings upon Muḥammad and the family of Muḥammad, just as You bestowed blessings upon the family of Ibrāhīm, You are the One full of praise, full of glory.'"

He also collected it in the Chapter of Supplications (*Da'awāt*) in his Ṣaḥīḥ, and Muslim collected this ḥadīth on the authority of Ka'b ibn 'Ujrah by way of several chains of transmission.

Also, al-Bukhārī collected in the Chapter of Supplications in his Ṣaḥīḥ on the authority of Abū Sa'īd al-Khudrī (رَضِيَ ٱللَّهُ عَنْهُ) who said: "We said: O Messenger of Allāh, this is the way to send Salām upon you, so how do we send Ṣalāt?" He said: 'Say:

اللَّهُمَّ صَلِّ عَلَى مُحَمَّدٍ عَبْدِكَ وَرَسُوْلِكَ كَمَا صَلَّيْتَ عَلَى إِبْرَاهِيمَ وَبَارِكْ على

مُحَمَّدٍ وآلِ مُحَمَّدٍ كَمَا بَارَكْتَ على إِبْرَاهِيمَ وَآلِ إِبْرَاهِيمَ

O Allāh send Ṣalāt upon Muḥammad, Your slave and Messenger, just as You sent Ṣalāt upon Ibrāhīm. And bestow blessings upon Muḥammad and the family of Muḥammad, just as You bestowed blessings upon Ibrāhīm and the family of Ibrāhīm.'"

[al-Bukhārī] also collected it from his narration under the Tafsīr of Sūrah al-Aḥzāb.

Also, al-Bukhārī reported in the "Book of Prophets" within his Ṣaḥīḥ on the authority of Abū Ḥumayd al-Sā'idī (رَضِيَ ٱللَّهُ عَنْهُ) that [the Companions] said: "O Messenger of Allāh, how do we send Ṣalāt upon you? So, the Messenger of Allāh (صَلَّى ٱللَّهُ عَلَيْهِ وَسَلَّمَ) said: 'Say:

اللَّهُمَّ صَلِّ عَلَى مُحَمَّدٍ وَأَزْواجِهِ وَذُرِّيَّتِهِ كَما صَلَّيْتَ عَلَى آلِ إِبْراهِيمَ وَبارِكْ على مُحَمَّدٍ وَأَزْواجِهِ وَذُرِّيَّتِهِ كَما بارَكْتَ على آلِ إبراهِيمَ إِنَّكَ حَمِيْدٌ مَجِيْدٌ

O Allāh send Ṣalāt upon Muḥammad and upon his wives and offspring, just as You sent Ṣalāt upon the family of Ibrāhīm. And bestow blessings upon Muḥammad and upon his wives and offspring, just as You bestowed blessings upon the family of Ibrāhīm, You are the One full of praise, full of glory.'"

He also collected upon his authority in the Chapter of Supplications what is similar to this wording, just as Imām Muslim collected this ḥadīth in his Ṣaḥīḥ on the authority of Abū Ḥumayd (رَضِيَ ٱللَّهُ عَنْهُ).

Also, Muslim collects in his Ṣaḥīḥ on the authority of Abū Mas'ūd al-Anṣarī who said: "The Messenger of Allāh (صَلَّى ٱللَّهُ عَلَيْهِ وَسَلَّمَ) came to us while we were in the sitting of Sa'd ibn 'Ubādah, so Bashīr ibn Sa'd said to him: 'Allāh the Most High has commanded us to send

Ṣalāt upon you, so how do we send Ṣalāt upon you?' [Abū Mas'ūd said]: The Messenger of Allāh (ﷺ) remained quiet up until the point we wished that we had not asked him. Then the Messenger of Allāh (ﷺ) said: 'Say:

اللَّهُمَّ صَلِّ عَلَى مُحَمَّدٍ وَعَلَى آلِ مُحَمَّدٍ كَمَا صَلَّيْتَ عَلَى إبْراهِيمَ وَبارِكْ على مُحَمَّدٍ وَعَلَى آلِ مُحَمَّدٍ كَما بارَكْتَ على آلِ إبْراهِيمَ فِي العالَمِيْنَ إِنَّكَ حَمِيْدٌ مَجِيْدٌ

O Allāh send Ṣalāt upon Muḥammad and the family of Muḥammad, just as You sent Ṣalāt upon Ibrāhīm. O Allāh bestow blessings upon Muḥammad and the family of Muḥammad, just as You bestowed blessings upon the family of Ibrāhīm throughout the creation, You are the One full of praise, full of glory.

And [sending] the Salām is as you have already learned.'"

These are the places in the two Ṣaḥīḥs —or one of them—where this ḥadīth has been collected. They were reported from four Companions: K'ab ibn 'Ujrah, Abū Sa'īd al-Khudrī, Abū Ḥumayd al-Sā'idī, and Abū Mas'ūd al-Anṣārī.

The narration of Ka'b and Abū Ḥumayd is agreed upon by al-Bukhārī and Muslim, while the narration of Abū Sa'īd is collected by al-Bukhārī alone, and the narration of Abū Mas'ūd al-Ansārī is collected by Muslim alone.

Others besides al-Bukhārī and Muslim have collected [this ḥadīth] from the narrations of these four [Companions]. Abū Dāwūd, al-Tirmidhī, al-Nasā'ī, Ibn Mājah, Imām Aḥmad, and al-Dārimī all collected it from the narration of Ka'b ibn 'Ujrah.

Al-Nasā'ī and Ibn Mājah both collected it from the narration of Abū Sa'īd al-Khudrī.

Abū Dāwūd, al-Nasā'ī, and Ibn Mājah collected it from the narration of Abū Ḥumayd.

Abū Dāwūd, al-Nasā'ī, and al-Dārimī collected it from the narration of Abū Mas'ūd al-Ansārī.

Furthermore, a group of Companions besides these four reported the ḥadīth describing the manner of sending Ṣalāt upon the Prophet (صَلَّى ٱللَّهُ عَلَيْهِ وَسَلَّمَ), from them: Ṭalḥa ibn 'Ubaydullāh, Abū Hurayrah, Buraydah ibn al-Ḥusayb, and Ibn Ma'sūd, may Allāh be pleased with them all.

The Best and Most Complete Manner of Sending Ṣalāt upon the Prophet (صَلَّى ٱللَّهُ عَلَيْهِ وَسَلَّمَ)

The manner in which the Prophet (صَلَّى ٱللَّهُ عَلَيْهِ وَسَلَّمَ) taught his Companions to send Ṣalāt upon him (صَلَّى ٱللَّهُ عَلَيْهِ وَسَلَّمَ) is the best manner of sending Ṣalāt upon him (صَلَّى ٱللَّهُ عَلَيْهِ وَسَلَّمَ). Additionally, the most complete form is that which combines between sending Ṣalāt upon the Prophet (صَلَّى ٱللَّهُ عَلَيْهِ وَسَلَّمَ) and his family, and Ibrāhīm and his family.

Al-Ḥāfiẓ ibn Ḥajar in *Fatḥ al-Bārī*, was from those who used the phrase which the Prophet (صَلَّى ٱللَّهُ عَلَيْهِ وَسَلَّمَ) taught his Companions, as proof that it is the best manner [of sending Ṣalāt upon him]. He said (11/166): "I say, it is proven, due to him (صَلَّى ٱللَّهُ عَلَيْهِ وَسَلَّمَ) teaching his Companions the manner [of sending Ṣalāt upon him] after their inquiry, that [his responses] are the best manner in sending Ṣalāt upon him. This is because he would not choose for himself except what is best and most noble. Hence, what comes as a result of this is that if one took an oath to send the best Ṣalāt upon [the Prophet], the way of fulfilling it is by saying [a supplication that he taught them]."

Subsequently, he mentioned that al-Nawawī deemed this to be correct in [his book] *al-Rawḍah*, and then he mentioned other ways by which one can fulfill an oath [taken in that regard]. He went on to say: "And what the evidences prove is that fulfilling [the oath taken in that regard] occurs through what has come in the ḥadīth of Abū Hurayrah (رَضِيَ ٱللَّهُ عَنْهُ), due to his saying: 'Whoever is pleased to take measurement with the most complete scale, then when he sends Ṣalāt upon us he says:

اللَّهُمَّ صَلِّ عَلَى مُحَمَّدٍ النَّبِيِّ وَأَزْوَاجِهِ أُمَّهاتِ المُؤْمِنِينَ وَذُرِّيَّتِهِ وَأَهْلِ بَيْتِهِ كَما صَلَّيْتَ عَلَى إبْراهِيمَ

O Allāh send Ṣalāt upon Muḥammad the Prophet, and his wives—the mothers of the believers—and his offspring and household, just as You sent Ṣalāt upon Ibrāhīm … to the end of the ḥadīth, and Allāh knows best.'"

Two Abridged Versions of Sending Ṣalāt and Salām Upon Him (ﷺ)

The pious predecessors (al-Salaf al-Ṣāliḥ), among them the scholars of ḥadīth (al-Muḥaddithūn), have commonly used two abridged phrases when mentioning the Ṣalāt and Salām upon [the Prophet] (ﷺ)

One: صَلَّى اللهُ عَلَيْهِ وَسَلَّمَ (May Allāh extol his mention and grant him goodness and well-being).

Two: عَلَيْهِ الصَّلاةُ وَالسَّلامُ (Upon him be the Ṣalāt of Allāh, goodness and well-being).

Praise be to Allāh, the books of ḥadīth are filled with these two [abridged] versions. Rather, in their books, the [scholars of ḥadīth] mention guidance concerning the strict preservation [of these sayings] in the most complete manner; and this is by combining sending Ṣalāt and Salām upon him (ﷺ).

In his book *'Ulūm al-Ḥadīth*, Imām Ibn al-Ṣalāḥ says: "It is incumbent upon him —meaning the one who writes ḥadīth— to strictly adhere to writing the Ṣalāt and Salām upon the Messenger of Allāh (ﷺ) when he is mentioned. He should not get tired of writing that down when [his name] is repeated. Surely, this is from the biggest benefits that the student and writer of ḥadīth will reap without delay. Consequently, whoever is negligent of this will prevent [himself] from a great portion [of goodness]...Also, when seeking to write it, he should avoid two blameworthy matters; **the first:** that he writes it in short-hand by abbreviating it with two letters or the like.[1] **Second:** that he writes it abbreviated in meaning, [for example] not writing وَسَلَّمَ ; even though this has been found in the writings of some early scholars."

Furthermore, al-Nawawī mentions in the book *al-Adhkār*: "If one of you sends Ṣalāt upon the Prophet (ﷺ), he should combine between sending both the Ṣalāt and Salām and not just suffice with one of them. Thus, he should not only say صَلَّى اللهُ عَلَيْهِ (May Allāh extol his mention) nor عَلَيْهِ السَّلَامُ (Upon him be goodness and well-being)."

Ibn Kathīr mentions at the end of his tafsīr of the verse in Sūrah al-Aḥzāb, expounding on [the statement of al-Nawawī]:

"What was said by [al-Nawawī] is derived from this verse, which is [Allāh's] statement:

﴿يَا أَيُّهَا الَّذِينَ آمَنُوا صَلُّوا عَلَيْهِ وَسَلِّمُوا تَسْلِيمًا ٥٦﴾

'O you who believe! Send your Ṣalāt on him and greet him with the Islāmic way of greeting.'

Based on this, it is foremost that it be said:

صَلَّى اللهُ عَلَيْهِ وَسَلَّمَ تَسْلِيمًا.

[1] **[TN]** Similar to how many people today write "Saws", "A.S." etc.

May Allāh extol his mention and grant him goodness and well-being in the best way."

Al-Fīrūz Ābādī stated in his book *Al-Ṣilāt wa al-Bushar*: "It is not befitting to abbreviate the Ṣalāt [upon the Prophet] as is done by some lazy individuals, the ignorant, and the laymen who seek knowledge. They write the abbreviation صَلْعَمْ instead of

صَلَّى اللهُ عَلَيْهِ وَسَلَّمَ.

The Virtue of Sending Ṣalāt Upon the Prophet (ﷺ)

Many aḥādīth have been reported concerning the virtue of sending Ṣalāt upon the Prophet (ﷺ). Al-Ḥāfiẓ Ismā'īl ibn Isḥāq al-Qāḍī designated a book solely to this subject. Also, in *Fatḥ al-Bārī*, when explaining the ḥadīth on the manner of sending Ṣalāt upon the Prophet (ﷺ) which al-Bukhārī collected in the Chapter of Supplications in his Ṣaḥīḥ; al-Ḥāfiẓ ibn Ḥajar alluded to [other] good standing narrations on the virtue of sending Ṣalāt upon the Prophet (ﷺ).

Al-Ḥāfiẓ ibn Ḥajar is from the [scholars] who possessed the ability to carefully examine texts [and extract benefits from knowledge-based matters], just as he was extremely well read in the books authored in the Prophetic Sunnah. Here, I will mention what he stated in this regard:

He said (رَحِمَهُ ٱللَّهُ): (11/167) "[This has been used] as proof for the virtue of sending Ṣalāt upon the Prophet (ﷺ), from the aspect that a command has been reported to do so, as well as the Companions showing concern by asking how it should be done. Furthermore, strong aḥādīth have been reported clearly stating its virtue–none of which have been collected by al-Bukhārī.

From them is what was collected by Muslim from the ḥadīth of Abū Hurayrah, attributing back [to the Prophet]:

من صلى عليّ واحدةً صلّى الله عليه عشراً

"Whoever sends one Ṣalāt upon me, Allah will send ten Ṣalāt upon him."

This also has a supporting [narration] from Anas collected by Aḥmad, and al-Nasā'ī, and was declared authentic by Ibn Ḥibbān; also, from Abū Burdah ibn Nayyār and Abū Ṭalḥa, both collected by al-Nasā'ī and their narrators are trustworthy. The wording of Abū Burdah's [narration] is:

من صلّى عليَّ من أمتي صلاة مخلصا من قلبه صلّى الله عليه بها عشر صلوات
ورفعه بها عشر درجات وكتب له بها عشر حسنات ومحا عنه عشر سيئات

'Whoever from my Ummah sends upon me a Ṣalāt sincerely from his heart, by it Allāh will send upon him ten Ṣalāt, raise him ten degrees, write for him ten good deeds, and remove from him ten bad deeds.'

The wording of Abū Ṭalḥa [in al-Nasā'ī] is similar to it and was authenticated by Ibn Ḥibbān.

There is also the ḥadīth of Ibn Mas'ūd attributing back [to the Prophet]:

إن أولى الناس بي يوم القيامة أكثرهم عليَّ صلاة

'Those who will have the best claim to me on the Day of Resurrection are those who send the most Ṣalāt upon me.'

This ḥadīth was declared as *ḥasan* by al-Tirmidhī and was authenticated by Ibn Ḥibbān.

Furthermore, it has a supporting narration collected by al-Bayhaqī on the authority of Abū Umāmah with the wording:

صلاة أمتي تعرض عليَّ في كل يوم جمعة فمن كان أكثرهم عليَّ صلاة كان أقربهم مني منزلة

'The Ṣalāt of my Ummah is presented to me every Friday. Whoever of them is most abundant in sending Ṣalāt upon me will be closest to me in station.'

It has a fair chain of narration.

Likewise, the command to be plentiful in sending Ṣalāt upon him on Friday has been reported from the ḥadīth of Aws ibn Aws, collected by Aḥmad and Abū Dāwūd and authenticated by Ibn Ḥibbān and al-Ḥākim.

Also, from that is the ḥadīth:

البخيل من ذكرت عنده فلم يصلِّ عليَّ

'The miser is the one who when I am mentioned in his presence, he does not send Ṣalāt upon me.'

This was collected by al-Tirmidhī, al-Nasā'ī, Ibn Ḥibbān, al-Ḥākim, and Ismā'īl al-Qāḍī who spoke at great length about its routes of transmission. He also clarified the differing that took place regarding it from the transmission of Alī and the ḥadīth of his son Ḥussain. Ultimately, the ḥadīth does not fall beneath the grade of *ḥasan.*

Also [from those narrations]:

من نسي الصلاة عليَّ خطئ طريق الجنة

'Whoever [intentionally] leaves off sending Ṣalāt upon me misses the path to Paradise.'

Collected by Ibn Mājah from the ḥadīth of Ibn Abbās, and by al-Bayhaqī in *al-Shu'ab* from the ḥadīth of Abū Hurayrah, Ibn Abī Ḥātim from the ḥadīth of Jābir, and al-Ṭabarānī from the ḥadīth of Ḥussain ibn Alī. All these chains of transmission strengthen one another.

There is another ḥadīth:

رَغِمَ أنفُ رجل ذكرت عنده فلم يصلِّ عليَّ

'May he be humiliated; the man when I am mentioned he does not send Ṣalāt upon me.'

And it was collected by al-Tirmdhī from the ḥadīth of Abū Hurayrah with the wording:

من ذكرت عنده فلم يصلِّ عليَّ فمات فدخل النار فأبعده الله

'The person who when I am mentioned and does not send Ṣalāt upon me; thus he dies and enters the Hellfire, may Allāh distance him.'

It has a supporting chain with [al-Tirmidhī] and was authenticated by al-Ḥākim. It also has a supporting chain from the narration of Abū Dharr in [the book of] al-Ṭabarānī and another from Anas collected by Ibn Abī Shaybah, and a third which is *mursal*[1] from al-Ḥasan (i.e. al-Baṣrī) collected by Sa'īd ibn Manṣūr.

It was likewise collected by Ibn Ḥibbān from the ḥadīth of Abū Hurayrah and Mālik ibn al-Ḥuwayrith. [Also,] from 'Abdullāh ibn 'Abbās which is in [the book of] al-Ṭabarānī, and from the ḥadīth of 'Abdullāh ibn Ja'far collected by al-Firyābī. [Furthermore], it is [collected] with al-Ḥākim from the ḥadīth of Ka'b ibn 'Ujrah with the wording:

بَعُدَ من ذكرت عنده فلم يصلِّ عليَّ

'May he be distanced; he who when I am mentioned in his presence, he does not send Ṣalāt upon me.'

It is also found in [the book of] al-Ṭabarānī from the ḥadīth of Jābir going back [to the Prophet]:

شَقِيَ عبد ذكرت عنده فلم يصلِّ عليَّ

'May he be wretched; the servant who when I am mentioned in his presence, he does not send Ṣalāt upon me.'

---

1 **[TN]** The *mursal ḥadīth* is when a *Tābi'ī* says: "The Messenger of Allāh said…" The general rule is that it is counted among the category of weak narrations as it is unknown whether the *Tābi'ī* heard the narration from a Companion or from other than a Companion. If supporting evidence is found from another route of transmission that is connected back to the Prophet (صَلَّى ٱللَّهُ عَلَيْهِ وَسَلَّمَ), then the *mursal ḥadīth* can be used as evidence.

It is also found with 'Abd al-Razzāq[1] from the *mursal* narration of Qatādah:

من الجفا أن أذكر عند رجل فلا يصلي عليَّ

'It is considered disaffection that I am mentioned in a man's presence, and he does not send Ṣalāt upon me.'

There is also the ḥadīth of Ubayy ibn Ka'b, that a man said: 'O Messenger of Allāh, I am plentiful in offering Ṣalāt, so what should I offer for you of my Ṣalāt? [The Prophet] said: 'Whatever you wish.' He said: 'A third?' [The Prophet] said: 'Whatever you wish, and if you increase this is better.' Up until the man said: 'I will offer for you all my Ṣalāt.' [The Prophet] said: 'Then you will be sufficed of your worries.'

This ḥadīth was collected by Aḥmad and others with a chain that is *ḥasan.*

So, these are the upstanding narrations which have been reported in this regard, and in this subject there are likewise many weak and unreliable narrations. As for what has been fabricated by the storytellers in this subject, they cannot be enumerated, and what we have of the strong narrations suffices us from [using] them." End of the words of al-Ḥāfiẓ ibn Ḥajar (رَحِمَهُ ٱللَّهُ).

Also, what is meant by Ṣalāt in the ḥadīth of Ubayy ibn Ka'b "so, what should I offer for you of my Ṣalāt" is du'ā'.[2]

---

[1] **[TN]** In his book *al-Muṣannaf*

[2] **[TN]** Meaning supplication, which is the original meaning of Ṣalāt in the Arabic language.

A Glimpse at Some Treatises Authored Surrounding Ṣalāt Upon the Prophet (صَلَّىٱللَّهُعَلَيْهِوَسَلَّمَ)

Indeed, the scholars have given importance to this tremendous act of worship, and [some] have dedicated works specifically to this topic. The first that I know having written concerning it is the Imām Ismā'īl ibn Isḥāq al-Qāḍī (D. 282H). The name of his book is *Faḍl al-Ṣalāt 'Alā al-Nabī* (صَلَّىٱللَّهُعَلَيْهِوَسَلَّمَ), and it was printed with the verification of Shaykh Muḥammad Nāṣir al-Dīn al-Albānī (رَحِمَهُٱللَّهُ). The treatise comprises of one-hundred and seven aḥādīth, all with their chains of narrations.

Also, from the books printed in this subject and in circulation is the book *Jilā al-Afhām Fī al-Ṣalāt wa al-Salām 'Alā Khayr al-Anām* by al-'Allāmah Ibn al-Qayyim, as well as the book *As-Ṣilāt Wa al-Bushar Fī al-Ṣalāt 'Alā Khayr al-Bashar* by al-Fīrūz Ābādī, the author of *al-Qāmūs*.[1] There is also the book *al-Qawl al-Badī Fī al-Ṣalāt 'Alā al-Ḥabīb al-Shafī'* by al-Sakhāwī (D. 902H). He concluded this book by mentioning a number of books regarding Ṣalāt upon the Prophet (صَلَّىٱللَّهُعَلَيْهِوَسَلَّمَ) in order. The fifth book [he mentioned] was *Jilā al-Afhām* by Ibn al-Qayyim. He alluded to some of the [knowledge-based] value of each book, then said: "In summary, the best of them and the most beneficial is the fifth book, meaning the book of Ibn al-Qayyim."

I say: In reality it is a very valuable book. In it, the author combined between mentioning the aḥādīth of the Prophet (صَلَّىٱللَّهُعَلَيْهِوَسَلَّمَ) concerning this great act of worship, and also refers to their authenticity or weakness, in addition to mentioning their

---

[1] **[TN]** A renowned Arabic dictionary. Its full title is *al-Qāmūs al-Muḥīṭ*.

proper understanding and what is derived from them of benefit. He said in its introduction: "It is a book unique in its subject. Nothing like it has come before it as it relates to the abundance of benefit. In it we clarified the aḥādīth reported concerning sending Ṣalāt and Salām upon him (صَلَّى ٱللَّهُ عَلَيْهِ وَسَلَّمَ), [distinguishing] what is authentic (*Ṣaḥīḥ*) from what is acceptable (*Ḥasan*) and what is weak (*Ma'lūl*), fully explaining the defects contained in the weak narrations. [We further explained] the subtleties contained in this du'ā, its nobility, and the wisdoms and benefits entailed in it. [Also,] the situations and places where Ṣalāt should be sent upon him (صَلَّى ٱللَّهُ عَلَيْهِ وَسَلَّمَ) and the amount [of Ṣalāt] which is obligatory [to be said]. [We mentioned] the differing of the people of knowledge regarding that, what is most preponderate [of their statements], and a mention of what is unreliable. [Ultimately], the content of the book is greater than what can be described, and all praise is for Allāh, Lord of all creation."

Furthermore, that which has been authored surrounding Ṣalāt upon the Prophet (صَلَّى ٱللَّهُ عَلَيْهِ وَسَلَّمَ), **based upon ignorance** and also entailing virtues and manners of sending Ṣalāt upon the Prophet (صَلَّى ٱللَّهُ عَلَيْهِ وَسَلَّمَ) which **[Allāh] sent down no authority**, is the book *Dalā'il al-Khayrāt*[1] by al-Jazūlī (D. 854H).

[This book] has gained repute and become widespread around the world. The author of *Kashf al-Thunūn* said concerning it (1/495): "*Dalā'il al-Khayrāt Wa Shawāriq al-Anwār Fī Dhikri al-*

---

[1] **[TN]** Sadly, this book has more than one translation in the English language. It has been printed under the title: DALĀ'ILU'L-KHAYRĀTI and: Guide to Goodness Dalā'il al-Khayrāt. On the cover of the latter, it is written "Great Books of the Islamic World", and this statement is deception and could not be further from the truth.

Ṣalāt 'Alā al-Nabī al-Mukhtār (عليه الصلاة والسلام), which begins with: 'All praise is due to Allāh who has guided us to faith...' by the Shaykh Abū 'Abdullāh Muḥammad ibn Abū Bakr al-Jazūlī al-Samlālī al-Sharīf al-Ḥasnī (d. 854H)...This book is one of the signs of Allāh concerning Ṣalāt upon the Prophet (ﷺ). It is constantly read in the East and West, especially in the Levant..."

Then he went on to mention some explanations of the book.

I say: The diligence shown by those great number of people in reciting [what is found in that book] is not based upon any firm foundation; it is only based upon the blind following the blind. Rather, the affair is just like Shaykh Muḥammad al-Khaḍr ibn Māya'bā al-Shinqīṭī stated in his book *Mushtahā al-Khārif al-Jāni Fī Radd Zalaqāt al-Tījānī al-Jānī*, while refuting al-Tījānī:

"People are infatuated with loving what is new and contemporary. For this reason, you see them always desiring the ṣalawāt reported in *Dalā'il al-Khayrāt* and [books] similar to it, and most [of those supplications] are void of an authentic chain. [At the same time] they turn away from the ṣalawāt reported from the Prophet (ﷺ) in Ṣaḥīḥ al-Bukhārī. Hence, you rarely find any scholars of virtue reciting any supplications [from the like of those deviant books]. [Those who are found doing so], it is only because of infatuation with what is new and contemporary. Had some virtue been anticipated from [those supplications], then no intelligent person —let alone a virtuous scholar— would turn away from [an authentically reported manner of] Ṣalāt upon the Prophet (ﷺ); [especially] after him being asked, 'how do we send Ṣalāt upon you O Messenger of Allāh?' And his response, 'say such and such...' He does not speak from his desires, but rather he speaks from revelation revealed to him. I say, [no intelligent person] would turn to [reciting] a Ṣalāt which is not supported by an authentic ḥadīth; or perhaps it is only supported by a dream of a man who *outwardly* is thought to be pious."

No doubt, what has been reported in the Sunnah and done by the noble Companions and those who followed them in goodness is the straight path and upright way. The benefit for the one who holds fast to that is guaranteed and harm is not expected to come to him. He (عليه الصلاة والسلام) said in a ḥadīth whose authenticity is agreed upon, [narrated] from 'Āishah (رَضِيَ اللَّهُ عَنْهَا):

من أحدث في أمرنا هذا ما ليس منه فهو ردٌّ

"Whoever introduces into this affair of ours (i.e. Islam) that which is not from it, it is rejected."

Also, in a narration [collected by] Muslim:

من عمل عملاً ليس عليه أمرنا فهو ردٌّ

"Whoever does an action not in accordance with our affair, it is rejected."

Furthermore, he (صَلَّى اللَّهُ عَلَيْهِ وَسَلَّمَ) said:

عليكم بسنتي وسنّة الخلفاء الراشدين المهديين من بعدي عضُّوا عليها
بالنواجذ وإياكم ومحدثات الأمور فإن كل محدثة بدعة وكل بدعة ضلالة

"Upon you is [to cling to] my Sunnah, and the Sunnah of the rightly guided Caliphs after me. Bite down upon [them both] with your molar teeth. And beware of newly invented matters, for every newly invented matter is an innovation, and every innovation is misguidance."

Also, he (عليه الصلاة والسلام) warned his Ummah from going to extremes concerning him. He said in the authentic ḥadīth:

لا تطروني كما أطرت النصارى ابن مريم إنما أنا عبد فقولوا عبد الله ورسوله

"Do not exaggerate concerning me as the Christians exaggerated concerning the son of Mary. I am merely a servant, therefore say [of me]: servant of Allāh and His Messenger."

Likewise, when a man said to him:

"Whatever Allāh and you will."

He (عليه الصلاة والسلام) said:

أجعلتني لله نِدّاً؟ ما شاء الله وحده

"Have you made me an equal alongside Allāh? It is whatever Allāh wills alone."

Hence, the book *Dalā'il al-Khayrāt* is mixed with good and bad and is conflated with what is permissible and prohibited. It has fabricated and weak narrations, entails exaggeration, and causes one to fall into impermissible matters which neither Allāh nor His Messenger (ﷺ) are pleased with. Furthermore, it is something novel, not upon the path of the righteous predecessors.

Innovated Manners of Supplication Found in the Book *Dalā'il al-Khayrāt*

Here, it is sufficient for me to allude to a few examples of some of the innovated manners of sending Ṣalāt and Taslīm upon the noble Prophet (ﷺ)–may Allāh bless him, his family, Companions, and those who follow them in goodness until the Day of Judgement. Then I will follow that up by mentioning some examples of fabricated narrations regarding the virtue of sending Ṣalāt upon him (ﷺ); words that his noble tongue is exalted from uttering.

Among the [innovated] manners [of supplication] found therein:

اللهم صل على محمد وعلى آل محمد حتى لا يبقى من الصلاة شيء وارحم محمدا وآل محمد حتى لا يبقى من الرحمة شيء وبارك على محمد وعلى آل محمد حتى لا يبقى من البركة شيء وسلم على محمد وعلى آل محمد حتى لا يبقى من السلام شيء

"O Allāh send Ṣalāt upon Muḥammad and the family of Muḥammad up until there remains no Ṣalāt. And have mercy upon Muḥammad and the family of Muḥammad up until there remains no mercy. And bestow blessings upon Muḥammad and the family of Muḥammad up until there remains no blessings. And send Salām upon Muḥammad and the family of Muḥammad up until there remains no Salām ."

His statement: "up until there remains no Ṣalāt, mercy, blessings, and Salām" is from the utmost despicable speech, and the utmost falsehood, because these actions do not come to an end.

And how can al-Jazūlī say: "up until there remains no mercy", when Allāh the Most High said:

﴿وَرَحْمَتِي وَسِعَتْ كُلَّ شَيْءٍ ۚ ﴿١٥٦﴾﴾

"And My mercy encompasses everything." Al-'Arāf 7:156.

Also, on page 71 he said:

اللهم صل على سيدنا محمد بحر أنوارك ومعدن أسرارك ولسان حجتك وعروس مملكتك وإمام حضرتك وطراز ملكك وخزائن رحمتك...إنسان عين الوجود والسبب في كل موجود

"O Allāh send Ṣalāt upon our chief Muḥammad, the ocean of Your lights, the treasure of Your secrets, the mouthpiece of Your proofs, the groom of Your kingdom, the leader of Your Exaltedness, the embroidery of Your dominion, and the treasure of Your mercy...he is the essence of existence and the purpose why everything is in existence."

And he said on page 64:

اللهم صل على من تفتقت من نوره الأزهار... اللهم صل على من اخضرت من بقية وضوئه الأشجار اللهم صل على من فاضت من نوره جميع الأنوار

O Allāh send Ṣalāt upon the one who, because of his light, the flowers sprout forth…O Allāh send Ṣalāt upon the one who, because of the remnants of his wuḍū, the trees turn green. O Allāh send Ṣalāt upon the one who, because of his light, all lights emanate.

These manners of supplication contain excessiveness which al-Muṣṭafā (ﷺ) is not pleased with, for verily it is he who said:

لا تطروني كما أطرت النصارى ابن مريم إنما أنا عبد فقولوا عبد الله ورسوله

"Do not exaggerate concerning me as the Christians exaggerated concerning the son of Mary. I am merely a servant, therefore say [of me]: servant of Allāh and His Messenger."

Collected by al-Bukhārī in his Ṣaḥīḥ.

Al-Jazūlī also stated on pages 144 and 145:

اللهم صل على محمد وعلى آل محمد ما سجعت الحمائم وحمت الحوائم

وسرحت البهائم ونفعت التمائم وشدت العمائم ونمت النوائم

"O Allāh send Ṣalāt upon Muḥammad and the family of Muḥammad so long as pigeons coo, and birds circle water [out of thirst], and animals graze, and amulets benefit, and turbans are wrapped, and living species grow."

His statement: "and amulets benefit" entails praising and encouraging amulets; [a matter] which he (ﷺ) forbade in his statement:

من تعلق تميمة فلا أتم الله له

"Whoever attaches an amulet [to himself], may Allāh not make his affairs successful."

Some Examples of Fabricated Aḥādīth in the Book *Dalā'il al-Khayrāt*

In what follows I will mention examples of fabricated or extremely weak aḥādīth found therein, while pointing out some of what was said by the people of knowledge regarding them. The intent here is to only highlight some of this; not that it is limited [to what will be mentioned].

He said on page 15: "It was reported that he (صَلَّى ٱللَّٰهُ عَلَيْهِ وَسَلَّمَ) said: 'Whoever sends one Ṣalāt upon me in order to glorify my right, Allāh (عَزَّوَجَلَّ) will create from that statement an angel with a wing in the East and another in the West whose feet is in the lowest seventh earth. His neck will [humbly] hang beneath the throne and Allāh (عَزَّوَجَلَّ) will say to him: send Ṣalāt upon My servant just as he sent Ṣalāt upon My Prophet. Thus [the angel] will send Ṣalāt upon him until the Day of Resurrection.'"

Also, he said on page 16: "And the Prophet (صَلَّى ٱللَّٰهُ عَلَيْهِ وَسَلَّمَ) said: 'There is no servant who sends Ṣalāt upon me except that the Ṣalāt will exit his mouth with haste and there will remain no land, sea, [direction of] East, or West except that it will pass by it and say: I am the supplication of so and so, son of so and so. He sent Ṣalāt upon Muḥammad, the chosen one; the best of Allāh's creation. So, there will not remain anything except it will send Ṣalāt upon him. And Allāh will create from that Ṣalāt a bird which has seventy thousand wings, on each wing there will be seventy thousand feathers, and on every feather will be seventy thousand faces. On every face there will be seventy thousand mouths and every mouth will have seventy thousand tongues. They will glorify

Allāh, the Most High, in seventy thousand languages, and Allāh will write for him the reward of all of that.'"

These two ḥadīths which are found in *Dalā'il al-Khayrāt* fall under what al-'Allāmah Ibn al-Qayyim (رَحِمَهُ ٱللَّهُ) stated in his book al-Manār al-Munīf when he said: "Fabricated ḥadīths are known to be overshadowed with darkness along with their feebleness in wording and foolish exaggeration, which [all] expose their fabrications and forgery."

He then mentioned some examples and afterwards said:

"Chapter: and here we will point out comprehensive principles by which it can be known that a ḥadīth is fabricated. From them: that it entails these foolish exaggerations; the like of which the Messenger of Allāh (صَلَّىٰ ٱللَّهُ عَلَيْهِ وَسَلَّمَ) will not utter. And they are many, such as what one of them said in a fabricated ḥadīth: 'Whoever says Lā ilāha illa Allāh, Allāh will create from that word a bird which has seventy thousand tongues, each tongue having seventy thousand languages which will seek Allāh's forgiveness for him.' And 'whoever does such and such they will be given seventy thousand cities in Paradise, in each city there will be seventy thousand palaces, in each palace there will be seventy thousand virgin women of Paradise'.

And other [narrations] which resemble these foolish exaggerations. The one who invents them is either one of two people; either one has who reached the pinnacle of ignorance and stupidity, or a heretic (zindīq) whose intention is to belittle the Messenger (صَلَّىٰ ٱللَّهُ عَلَيْهِ وَسَلَّمَ) by attributing these [foolish] statements to him."

Also, from the contemporary commentators who pointed out the falsity of these narrations is Abū al-Faḍl 'Abdullāh ibn al-Siddīq al-Ghumārī, who stated in his commentary upon the book: *Bishārat al-Maḥbūb bi Takfīr al-Dhunūb* by al-Adhraʿī (p. 125) "Notice: It has been reported in many aḥādīth: whoever does such and such, Allāh will create from that action an angel to glorify or praise Allāh, and all of them are false aḥādīth."

This is his statement here, but [strangely] he highly praised *Dalā'il al-Khayrāt* in his book *Khawāṭir Dīnīyyah* and described it as having traveled the journey of the sun.[1]

---

[1] **[TN]** This is an exaggerated statement from al-Ghumārī which clearly contradicts what he said in the commentary of the book: *Bishārat al-Maḥbūb bi Takfīr al-Dhunūb* by al-Adhraʿī.

The Great Status of the Sunnah Among the Salaf and a Clarification of Why They Were Victorious Over Their Enemies, Contrary to the Condition of the Muslims Today

It pleases me to end this talk by relaying a portion of what I wrote in explanation of the ḥadīth of Ka'b ibn 'Ujrah (رَضِيَٱللَّهُعَنْهُ) regarding the manner of sending Ṣalāt upon the Prophet (صَلَّىٱللَّهُعَلَيْهِوَسَلَّمَ). It is the nineteenth ḥadīth from the twenty that I selected from Ṣaḥīḥ Muslim and printed with the title: '*Ishrūna Ḥadīthan Min Ṣaḥīḥi Muslim Dirāsat Asānīdihā Wa Sharḥu Mutūnihā*[1]:

The statement of Ka'b ibn 'Ujrah (رَضِيَٱللَّهُعَنْهُ) to Ibn Abī Laylā: 'Shall I not gift you with a gift..." This shows that the aḥādīth of the Messenger of Allāh (صَلَّىٱللَّهُعَلَيْهِوَسَلَّمَ), knowing his Sunnah (صَلَّىٱللَّهُعَلَيْهِوَسَلَّمَ), and implementing it was the most precious and most beloved things to their souls. For this reason, Ka'b made this statement, highlighting the importance of what he was going to relay to Ibn Abī Laylā, in order that he could prepare himself to understand it, receive it, and thoroughly comprehend it.

Moreover, because the Salaf gave great importance to the Sunnah of their Prophet (صَلَّىٱللَّهُعَلَيْهِوَسَلَّمَ) and were eager to [learn it], and it was their most valuable gift —due to what their hearts held of love for it and eagerness to implement it— they became the elites among the rest of the nations and were those the world looked upon [with respect]. Victory over their enemies became their familiar companion, and strength and power was in the favor of Islām and its people. Just as Allāh, the Most High said:

---

[1] **[TN]** Its translated meaning: *Twenty Ḥadīths from Ṣaḥīḥ Muslim: A study of their chains and an explanation of their texts.*

﴿إِن تَنصُرُوا اللَّهَ يَنصُرْكُمْ وَيُثَبِّتْ أَقْدَامَكُمْ ﴿٧﴾﴾

"If you help (in the cause of) Allāh, He will help you, and make your foothold firm." Muḥammad 47:7

This is contrary to what we see today of the sad reality of the Muslims; [we see] the forsaking of one another, separation, abandoning the lofty teachings of the religion and remaining distant from it —except those who Allāh has bestowed mercy on— and they are exceptionally rare. So, because of their state, their enemies consider them as absolutely nothing and do not respect them in the slightest. [The Muslims] have become those who are fearful while their predecessors were feared. Their enemy has waged attacks upon them in the midst of their own land, and [unfortunately], by their own children who were educated among [the enemy].

Therefore, if the intelligent one ponders over what this noble ḥadīth entails in clarification of the sheer pricelessness of the prophetic Sunnah within the souls of the pious predecessors, and its tremendous status among them, and how it was their most precious gift; then he looks at the condition of many of those who ascribe to Islām today and how they have been tested with abandoning the Islāmic legislation and returning to other than it for judgment…I say, if the intelligent one ponders over the condition of the former and the condition of those today, he will grasp the secret behind why the former gained victory over their enemies, although they were fewer in number and armaments; whereas [the Muslims today] are defeated, while they have great numbers in front of their enemies.

Consequently, the Muslims will never become triumphant unless they return back to the Mighty Book and the purified Sunnah, discarding the lowly man-made laws and the overflow of filth which is imported from foreign lands, and then cleanse their lands and themselves from all of that.

I ask Allāh the Generous, Lord of the Mighty Throne to grant all the Muslims success —both rulers and subjects— to return to the Book of their Lord, and the Sunnah of their Prophet Muḥammad (ﷺ). This is so that they may attain the true means to victory and triumph over their enemies. Indeed, He is the All-Hearer and the One who answers the supplications. And All praise is due to Allāh, Lord of all creation.

اللَّهُمَّ صَلِّ عَلَى مُحَمَّدٍ وَعَلَى آلِ مُحَمَّدٍ كَمَا صَلَّيْتَ عَلَى إِبْرَاهِيمَ وَعَلَى آلِ إِبْرَاهِيمَ إِنَّكَ حَمِيْدٌ مَجِيْدٌ اللَّهُمَّ بَارِكْ عَلَى مُحَمَّدٍ وَعَلَى آلِ مُحَمَّدٍ كَمَا بَارَكْتَ عَلَى إِبْرَاهِيمَ وَعَلَى آلِ إِبْرَاهِيمَ إِنَّكَ حَمِيْدٌ مَجِيْدٌ

O Allāh send Ṣalāt upon Muḥammad and the family of Muḥammad, just as You sent Ṣalāt upon Ibrāhīm and the family of Ibrāhīm, You are the One full of praise, full of glory. O Allāh bestow blessings upon Muḥammad and the family of Muḥammad, just as You bestowed blessings upon Ibrāhīm and the family of Ibrāhīm, You are the One full of praise, full of glory.